Dedicated to Lord Ganesha and Lord Krishna

5 KEY TAKEAWAYS FROM BHAGAWAD GITA

AKILAN R

ISBN 979-888606236-6

Contents

Foreword

Preface

Srimad Bhagawad Gita (**BG**) - the very mention of this brings to our mind that lots of famous personalities throughout the world have written commentaries from time immemorial. It is quite a long list of such names starting from Adi Shankara, and to understand his commentary on BG, we need an exhaustive and thorough knowledge of Sanskrit. It is also translated in various languages of the world.

The beauty of BG is such it is relevant even in the 21st Century when humans have attained scientific advancements in almost every field of their endeavors.

In my attempt to decode the underlying principles from BG, I have taken references from various content published on the internet and discussed in various popular forums, blogs etc. I don't want to attempt any translation for this great work and I have to admit that I don't have the necessary knowledge and experience to do so.

It is only my sincere and humble effort to highlight and discuss only 5 Key Takeaways from the immense knowledge discussed through Q&A sessions between Lord Sri Krishna the God Incarnate of Lord Vishnu and one of the great warriors of mankind, Arjuna.

But the context in which this conversation took place is where Bhagawat Gita stands distinct from other texts. War was about to begin any time and entire armies from either side of Pandavas and Kauravas were just waiting for the Conch to be blown signaling the start of the great war. Arjuna requested Krishna to take the chariot so that he could see the forces lined up and ready to fight the battle. When he saw that great kings and his own teacher and one of the most revered Bishma was commanding the opposite side, his inner strength and will power was totally shattered and he dropped his bows and arrows thinking it would be a sinful act to kill his own cousins and other great men from Kaurava camp. Lord Krishna on seeing Arjuna's plight and inhibition immediately understood and reacted swiftly to motivate Arjuna taking lots of references from Vedas and Upanishads. He did it in an extempore manner and patiently listening to Arjuna's questions and answered all of them with courage and conviction.

Even though all five Takeaways are explained as separate chapters, it is to be noted that they are all linked to one another and need to be seen from a holistic perspective. The idea is not to quote a word to word translation of the entire BG but only a handful of key criteria hidden inside this vast treasure, analyze and explain with the modern ideas of modern-day philosophers.

Acknowledgements

Dedicating this book to my friends, mentors and internet Gurus and to my family

CHAPTER ONE

Be Yourself

"To be yourself in a world that is constantly trying to make you something else is the greatest accomplishment." —**Ralph Waldo Emerson**

Sir Ken Robinson relates many such stories in his path-breaking work *The Element* (2009). His fundamental observation is that people are "in the element" when natural aptitude meets personal passion. He goes on to speak about how it involves being connected with like-minded people, gently pushing away criticism (that is often well-meaning), and finding mentors along the way. He also assures us that age is no bar to get into the element.

BG, composed several thousands of years earlier, surprisingly says something very similar, but with a slightly different spin, as we will see a little later.

Each of us is endowed with several abilities to varying degrees of competence. We also have different passions to varying degrees of interest. With some effort and experimentation, we should be able to find that sweet spot where we are deeply attracted to something that we are really good at. This is the beginning of personal success, which eventually leads to the creation of something remarkable, something so truly "us". Given that each of us is unique, if we stuck with ourselves instead of copying others, we'd be able to offer something unique to society.

All this sounds rather straightforward. But people are still afraid of following their passions into the dark and mysterious alleys it may lead them to. One of the reasons is that our society has already identified a few professions that are safe. If one aspires to be an engineer or a lawyer or a doctor, the chances of getting a decent job are high. If one aspires to be an art historian or a philosopher or a poet, the chances are not as good. Further, society slots the well-paying professions as the better ones. Quite naturally, our role models are men and women from one of these chosen professions.

In spite of this, the new generation of entrepreneurs, writers, social workers, and wildlife conservationists have followed their calling. Perhaps they did so because it was impossible not to be themselves. It was impossible not to give expression to their real nature. And by doing this, they not only found inner peace but also became valuable to the world.

This trend started much earlier in the West. Perhaps with the advent of the self-esteem movement in the US, more and more young men and women began asserting themselves and followed through on their convictions instead of blindly following the herd. There is a famous prose-poem by Virginia Satir called *My Declaration of Self-Esteem* (1975), which epitomizes the ideas of this movement. She says, "In all the world, there is no one else exactly like me. Everything that comes out of me is authentically me. Because I alone chose it - I own everything about me. My body, my feelings, my mouth, my voice, all my actions, whether they be to others or to myself. I own my fantasies, my dreams, my hopes, my fears..." Perhaps this reminds you of something in the recent past. But first let's see what the Bhagavad Gita says.

In the 18th chapter, there is an exceptional verse (18.46) in which Krishna tells Arjuna: "One finds fulfillment by working in harmony with his natural abilities and making that as an offering to the One, who pervades this universe and from whom all creatures have arisen." In the next verse, Krishna speaks about working in tune with one's temperament and interests instead of trying to imitate others - an attempt that inevitably leads to guilt and sorrow.

Clothed in different words and an other-worldly idiom is precisely the idea that Sir Ken Robinson so brilliantly espouses in his book. But with a twist. Why does Krishna ask Arjuna to make "that as an offering to the One that pervades the universe"? Krishna could have directly asked Arjuna to dedicate his actions to god, but he doesn't. He not only refers to god as the one that "pervades this universe" but also as the one "from whom all creatures have arisen". Krishna's choice of words is significant, especially when we look at the downside of the self-esteem movement.

Humans are inexorably connected with nature, society, community, and family. Thus it becomes essential that each one of us is aware of the possible consequences of our actions on our immediate surroundings, if not the society at large. While my passions are important for me, another person's passion is important for him/her - indeed such mindfulness will bring about mutual nourishment and harmony.

Being yourself is the most important skill you can ever possess. When you know who you are, you know what you need to do, instead of looking for permission from others to do what you already know you ought to do. It allows you to eliminate tons of frustration caused by wasting time on the wrong things.

Quit when you've put in ample time and your efforts aren't giving back in return. What is ample time? Only you can decide that. But when you quit correctly, it isn't giving up, it's making room for something better. When your actions do nothing but drain you—rather than produce more passion and increase your drive to do more—that's a good sign it is time to focus elsewhere

Following the passion. It indicates an area of life that you need to pay more attention to. If we're talking about following your passion in work, it's a good thing. And if we're talking about having more passion for life, it's a good thing. Focus more on passion; understand yourself in better ways, and you'll make a bigger impact. Passion produces effort and continuous effort produces results.

A large aspect of being yourself can be found in your relationships. When you realize you'll never truly know anyone else until you discover being yourself, the importance of being yourself becomes even more apparent. This especially rings true for business leaders, because if they don't know the people on their team, then he/she will fail as a leader. But this rule also applies to any relationship in your life. Almost as much as you need to know yourself, other people also need to know who you are. People need you—the real you.

Use your reflections to fight your biggest fears, because when you understand who you are meant to be, your purpose will finally become bigger than your fears. When you realize who you are, you will spend less time spinning your wheels. Focusing on your strengths gives you the needed traction to begin making a bigger and better difference in the world. When you know yourself, you will find more peace, and you will find success quicker than ever before.

Once you realize being yourself, you will become more confident, you will understand your purpose, and you will begin making a bigger impact on the world.

Thus the crux of BG can be summarized only with 2 words, the opening word "Dharma" (meaning law of being) from the first verse and the last word "Mama" of Chapter 18-Verse78 (meaning My), roughly this translates to "Be Yourself" in English.

CHAPTER TWO

Be A Smart Worker

"The most successful men work smart, not hard"
— Bangambiki Habyarimana, The Great Pearl of Wisdom

BG is unique in its contribution to the philosophy of pragmatic living:

Let your concern (or focus) be on your action, let it not be on the outcome of the action. Do not act only out of expectation of a result, but then do not slip into inactivity." (Chapter2:47)

Detach yourself from the fruits of your actions

As an entrepreneur, the decision to not work for someone else and instead make a name for oneself can stem from different motivations, including gaining wealth, becoming famous, or indulging in a new way of life.

These motivations slowly will become expectations. With every action that you take, say, attend a meeting with an investor, or release your product for beta-testing, you start expecting some positive results. The reality, however, as you might have realized, is different. Just a single action does not yield a positive outcome.

It takes a long time for your actions to compound and become large and impactful enough to drive any kind of positive change to grow your enterprise. Only with multiple meetings with the investor or continuous revisions to the product's features and UX can reasonable expectations come. Months of hard work need to turn into years of dedication before an entrepreneur can see any fruitful results.

Never let the results directly influence your actions

This lesson takes the idea of not being attached to results, a step further. For a normal person working a stable job, life consists of a series of successes and failures. We feel happy when we experience success, and sad during failure. This is quite normal.

But the journey of an entrepreneur is like a rollercoaster ride, with multiple ups and downs that have no gaps in between for breathing. If the entrepreneur also experiences these successes and failures in the same way as a normal person, then their mental health would be completely wrecked.

That is why it is advisable to treat every success and failure equally, and never letting the results of any actions, e.g., an investment or a successful launch or an unstable quarter, directly affect your dedication to work.

Don't allow external factors to affect your dedication

When one is neither attached to sense objects nor to actions, that person is said to be elevated in the science of Yoga, for having renounced all desires for the fruits of actions.

Sense-objects are the things experienced by your sensory organs; normally known as external factors. The entrepreneur is continuously hit by external factors— a personal commitment that makes them cancel important meetings or sickness that doesn't allow them to perform at their peak. Such factors do slow down progress and hinder growth.

But the entrepreneur needs to realize that such things are unavoidable and importantly, uncontrollable. Getting frustrated because of such external factors brings no solutions at all. By not letting external factors dictate one's mood, one can focus on remedying the problematic situation instead of getting bothered by it.

Recognize the natural state of your mind

Elevate yourself through the power of your mind, and not degrade yourself, for the mind can be the friend and also the enemy of the self.

While entrepreneurs can claim that they know their employees or competitors well enough, they cannot do the same for themselves. Entrepreneurs are a busy set of people, always surrounded by other people and their needs. Their focus is always on the outside: "Is there a new competitor?" or "How can I get more investors interested in my enterprise?" They are always lost in the thoughts that are bound outside of their physical being, and most times, they forget to pay attention to their bodies and their minds. They might eat less, sleep less, or work harder than they should. Such habits are, however, the leading causes for early burnouts.

You, the entrepreneur, are the most vital asset to your enterprise. Just as how you assess the performance and well-being of your employees, you need to assess yourself as well. The greatest entrepreneurs have always been introspective for the same reason. They know that to be at the top of their performance, they need to monitor how they feel. Along with this, they should not let any kind of failure demotivate their overall energetic spirits.

One easy way to remember this is to quote the Greek: "Know Thyself"

Form habits to elevate your natural state

For those who have conquered the mind, it is their friend. For those who have failed to do so, the mind works like an enemy. This lesson moves forward from the idea of knowing one's natural state. While Rome might not have been built in a single day, it was definitely built on actions done by people on a daily basis. Whether it is from the viewpoint of the physical city itself that needs bricks to be laid and roads to be paved, or the viewpoint of the empire that grew only because the emperors were never satisfied and continued to war and conquer; whatever they did, they did it every single day.

While the emperors' habits were productive, some of the entrepreneur's might not be. It could take the form of overthinking or feeling anxious every time they reach out to a new prospect. Since habits help make our daily activities automatic, we do not often realize when we perform them. This lack of self-awareness can be detrimental, as bad habits (such as overthinking) lead to decreased productivity. However, making a habit out of always monitoring how one feels and acts can help solve that.

To quote the Greek again, "We are what we repeatedly do. Excellence, then, is not an act, but a habit", said Aristotle.

Everything is cyclic in the world.

If you become successful, start giving back to the work. Actions based upon the sacrifice, charity, and penance should never be abandoned; they must certainly be performed. Indeed, acts of sacrifice, charity, and penance are purifying even for those who are wise.

The soil allows plants to grow, whose fruits we consume. When we die, we bury our bodies into the same soil, nourishing it. This is the cycle of life. Similarly, everything that keeps our hyper-modernized world running is part of a cycle, especially the world's economy.

A new, well-thought business with skilled employees will grow, flourish, and make the founders rich and the investors richer. The mere existence of this new business creates more jobs, moving many people forward in their lives. But with great success comes great responsibility. Merely celebrating one's success all alone does not help the entire world to become better. As an entrepreneur gains more fame, they should start contributing to the community that surrounds them. The entrepreneur could spend time training the younger generation and passing on the skills and knowledge that made them successful.

Not everything is important. Give priority to prioritizing.

The intellect is said to be in the nature of goodness, O Parth, when it understands what is proper action and what is improper action, what is duty and what is non-duty, what is to be feared and what is not to be feared, what is binding and what is liberating.

The human mind is like a horse galloping through the forest without any master on its reins. We think about a thousand things in a single minute: how other people judge us, what can we have for dinner, and so on. And as observed above, the entrepreneur is always surrounded by people. This means that people would bring their thousand thoughts to you.

While you are the most vital asset to your company, your time is your most vital asset. Whatever that actually needs your immediate focus, such as a call with a huge client, should be prioritized. Other things such as reassuring a customer that does not significantly contribute to your profits and just complains, can be attended to later.

Don't let your passion dictate your actions.
The intellect is considered in the mode of passion when it is confused between righteousness and unrighteousness, and cannot distinguish between right and wrong conduct.

When someone or something is very close to our hearts, we become blind to their biggest faults because of our love. We go on and always highlight their positive qualities. If someone dares to speak a word against our loved things, we get defensive. Such can happen with an entrepreneur as well if he/she gets too close to a project. For all the time, energy, and mental commitment that they pour into it, it is bound to happen.

But such attachment should not be encouraged. The entrepreneur should never let emotions get involved in the way of making informed decisions. If a product constantly fails in the market despite several revamps, it should be removed from the market and scrapped. Maintaining it just because of a personal affection toward it will only create more losses. It could also affect relationships with other collaborators who do not see the value in keeping a failing product alive.

Be determined to destroy any sort of an obstacle.
The steadfast will that is developed through Yog, and which sustains the activities of the mind, the life-airs, and the senses, is said to be determination in the mode of goodness. Can you guess the most vital asset of an enterprise? It has been repeated twice, so it is pretty simple to recall: The entrepreneur. And while he/she might have a lot of skills, experience, connections, and valuable employees, the steering wheel driving their dreams is their willpower or determination.

When a person embarks on the journey of entrepreneurship, they have many expectations. As they keep sailing forward, they are hit by many problems. The first product might fail, the capital might run out, or the best employees might leave. It is only the determination of the entrepreneur to still try again, to build another product, to seek more investors, that keeps their ship floating during any storm.

Rely on yourself more than you do others.

That which seems like poison at first, but tastes like nectar in the end, is said to be happiness in the mode of goodness. It is generated by the pure intellect that is situated in self-knowledge.

Taking the previous idea forward, this lesson encourages the entrepreneur to believe and rely on the crucial asset of their enterprise: themselves. There are only a few people who believe in the idea that sparked the beginning of a business— the founders, and maybe their families. To move their business forward, they would have to pursue and convince other people to believe in their vision. So, during the very first days of the business, all the work is done by solely them.

Now, if there is just one founder for an enterprise, then there is no one he/she can rely on during the initial stages. Employees that join during such stages mostly leave whenever they feel that the enterprise is not doing well, and initial investors might pull back if they feel that the profits aren't enough. The single entrepreneur ends up being with just themselves, having to deal with everything alone.

If the entrepreneur understands the fact that they might have to deal with the worst all alone, from the very beginning, then that frames every decision that they take and makes them stronger.

As an entrepreneur, tough situations can often lead to dilemmas that jam the brain. These lessons from the Gita are bound to help your way through them.

The core of these lessons boils down to : Relying on your self and steps to a smart worker. Every other idea shows how to transform one's inner self into a more resilient one in the face of distractions.

In short, know what you are capable of, set goals to turn the capability into opportunities, and start putting in effort in the long run. That sums up the path to a smart worker

CHAPTER THREE

Be Self Aware

"*Your visions will become clear only when you can look into your own heart. Who looks outside, dreams; who looks inside, awakes.*" - **C.G. Jung**

Self-awareness seems to have become the latest management buzzword — and for good reason. Research suggests that when we see ourselves clearly, we are more confident and more creative. We make great decisions, build stronger relationships, and communicate more effectively. We're more-effective leaders with more-satisfied employees and more-profitable companies.

Self-awareness is a fundamental quality to living an effective, empowered, and fulfilling life. Being aware or conscious of and reliant upon your own powers and abilities is what allows you to think, speak, and act purposefully and believe that you have the inner strength and courage to succeed.

Like everyone, there are times you can lose confidence in yourself and slip into bouts of doubt, insecurity, and uncertainty. Lacking self-confidence, you may fear and suspect that you are weak or incompetent and thereby hesitate to speak or act with assertiveness, missing out on potential opportunities for growth or success. You may sabotage and hold yourself back in your work, relationships, or personal life. As anyone who has slipped into ruts of self-doubt and insecurity can tell you, this is not a pleasant state to be in. So how can you maintain a healthy level of self-confidence in who you are and what you can do?

Self-awareness helps managers identify gaps in their management skills, which promotes skill development. But self-awareness also helps managers find situations in which they will be most effective, assists with intuitive decision making, and aids stress management and motivation of oneself and others.

Skill development.

Improvement projects should normally begin with an assessment of the gap between the current situation and the desired future situation. Having an accurate sense of who you are helps you decide what you should do to improve. Often, self-awareness will reveal a skills gap that you want to work on.

Knowing your strengths and weaknesses. Self-awareness helps you exploit your strengths and cope with your weaknesses. For instance, if you are someone who is good at "seeing the big picture" that surrounds decisions, but not as good at focusing on the details, you might want to consult colleagues and subordinates that are more detail-oriented when making major decisions. Cooperation between big-picture-oriented decision makers and detail-oriented decision makers can produce high quality decisions.

Developing intuitive decision-making skills.

Leaders with well-developed emotional self-awareness are more effective intuitive decision makers. In complex situations, intuitive decision makers process large amounts of sometimes unstructured and ambiguous data, and they choose a course of action based on a "gut feeling" or a "sense" of what's best. This type of decision making is becoming more important for managers as the rate of change and the levels of uncertainty and complexity in their competitive environments increase. Managers who are highly emotionally self-aware are better able to read their "gut feelings" and use them to guide decisions.

Stress. Jobs that don't suit your personality tend to give you more stress than jobs that are more compatible. This is not to say that you should never take a job that conflicts with your personality. However, be aware that you will need to work extra hard to develop the skills for that job, and there are jobs that would be less stressful for you.

Motivation. It's very difficult to cope with poor results when you don't understand what causes them. When you don't know what behaviors to change to improve your performance, you just feel helpless. Self-awareness is empowering because it can reveal where the performance problems are and indicate what can be done to improve performance. In addition, awareness of your psychological needs can increase your motivation by helping you understand and seek out the rewards that you really desire such as a sense of accomplishment, additional responsibility, an opportunity to help others, or a flexible work schedule.

Leadership. When we understand "what make us tick"--what gets us excited, why we behave the way we do, etc.--we also have insight into what makes others tick. To the extent that other people are like you (and, of course, there are limits to the similarity), knowing how to motivate yourself is tantamount to knowing how to motivate others.

Excellent inspiring Quotes on Self-Awareness :

"As you become more clear about who you really are, you'll be better able to decide what is best for you, the first time around." - **Oprah Winfrey**

"Without self-awareness we are as babies in the cradles." - **Virginia Woolf**

"Self-awareness is not just relaxation and not just meditation. It must combine relaxation with activity and dynamism." - **Deepak Chopra**

"Self-awareness is the ability to take an honest look at your life without any attachment to it being right or wrong, good or bad." - **Debbie Ford**

"I think self-awareness is probably the most important thing towards being a champion." - **Billie Jean King**

"Self-awareness is one of the rarest of human commodities. I don't mean self-consciousness where you're limiting and evaluating yourself. I mean being aware of your own patterns." - **Tony Robbins**

CHAPTER FOUR

Be the Best

"*You were born to win, but to be a winner, you must plan to win, prepare to win, and expect to win.*"

— Zig Ziglar"

When you walk your talk and do the right things, it makes your world a better place, both for you and for those you care about. It's not about wanting other people to think and act the way you do; it's about being tolerant and keeping a proper perspective. The idea here is to be your best self without compromising your values. You'll feel better for it, as will others around you.

If you feel that what's good for the people you love is also good for you, then you've created a balanced life. Envy is never part of the equation. Seeing a friend, loved one, or business associate succeed should bring a feeling of joy. People who possess this quality know that the good that comes to others will also affect them in a positive way. They also believe in helping people, for they know that doing this just makes your circle (of people and influence) stronger.

Being a good person also means giving others the room they need to be themselves, even if you don't agree with some of their actions. All you can do is be the best you can be and hope that other people see it, like it, and want to emulate it. Knowing the outcome of putting out positive energy makes it easier to do and also gives you the sense that your purpose in life is greater than you may have suspected.

When you enjoy doing the right thing and don't expect much in return, you actually get a lot back. Teaching others to "pay it forward" and being an example of that ideal is another way you can use who you are to make changes in the people you touch, each and every day.

When you employ the attitude of being your best self, and your focus is toward the highest good, your sense of who you really are will get stronger, and you will get more out of life. You will get a wonderful feeling from doing the right thing. This feeling is unmistakable and can come from taking action to help those in need or from making the world a tiny bit better in any way you can.

Living your life in the best way possible is a win-win. Being here just for yourself is unfulfilling. It's how we all pull together that makes the world a better place. I really don't know how else to do it. Getting an entire planet on the same page isn't really possible, so I think it best to do all you can in your own little corner of the globe and trust that your actions will spill over and have a positive effect on many.

When you walk your talk and do the right things, it makes your world a better place, both for you and for those you care about. It's not about wanting other people to think and act the way you do; it's about being tolerant and keeping a proper perspective. The idea here is to be your best self without compromising your values. You'll feel better for it, as will others around you.

If you feel that what's good for the people you love is also good for you, then you've created a balanced life. Envy is never part of the equation. Seeing a friend, loved one, or business associate succeed should bring a feeling of joy. People who possess this quality know that the good that comes to others will also affect them in a positive way. They also believe in helping people, for they know that doing this just makes your circle (of people and influence) stronger.

Being a good person also means giving others the room they need to be themselves, even if you don't agree with some of their actions. All you can do is be the best you can be and hope that other people see it, like it, and want to emulate it. Knowing the outcome of putting out positive energy makes it easier to do and also gives you the sense that your purpose in life is greater than you may have suspected.

When you enjoy doing the right thing and don't expect much in return, you actually get a lot back. Teaching others to "pay it forward" and being an example of that ideal is another way you can use who you are to make changes in the people you touch, each and every day.

When you employ the attitude of being your best self, and your focus is toward the highest good, your sense of who you really are will get stronger, and you will get more out of life. You will get a wonderful feeling from doing the right thing. This feeling is unmistakable and can come from taking action to help those in need or from making the world a tiny bit better in any way you can.

Living your life in the best way possible is a win-win. Being here just for yourself is unfulfilling. It's how we all pull together that makes the world a better place. I really don't know how else to do it. Getting an entire planet on the same page isn't really possible, so I think it best to do all you can in your own little corner of the globe and trust that your actions will spill over and have a positive effect on many.

References from Harward Business Review

in 2005, a Harvard Business Review article was published which introduced a new approach to personal and professional development: the idea that receiving affirmation is a powerful way for us to grow, particularly when it comes in the form of stories describing moments when we are at our best. In this article the Reflected Best Self Exercise (RBSE), a tool based on our academic research was introduced which is now used by thousands of people globally in corporate trainings, team building, executive leadership programs, and in graduate and undergraduate courses in a variety of disciplines.

Research stemming from this work shows that people benefit significantly from positive feedback about their strengths and contributions. It fosters healthy emotions, builds personal agency and resourcefulness, and helps to strengthen the quality of our relationships with colleagues, friends and family members. Sharing information about our reflected best selves with new colleagues as a part of onboarding processes also increases job satisfaction and reduces employee turnover.

Going through the full Reflected Best Self Exercise itself provides concentrated, if infrequent, dose of positive feedback. But there are organic ways that you can learn about and activate your best self at work every day as well. We've seen this more continual approach help people find new opportunities to develop parts of themselves that get lost in the daily demands of work, notice new ways of crafting their jobs, or take new steps towards longed-for callings. This article highlights five practices for noticing and capitalizing on everyday opportunities for development based on your best self.

Notice Positive Feedback

Most people are well-attuned to critical feedback; it is jarring, threatening, and emotional, and as a result, quite memorable. In contrast, it is often easy to let positive reflections on our actions subtly slip us by. Lingering in the glow of praise can also feel uncomfortably immodest. It therefore takes practice to savor moments of positivity and to hold them in your memory.

To capture these moments, create a space (digital or physical) where you save any positive feedback that you receive. This could include thank-you notes, comments written in your formal evaluations, or references to your work in email threads. And don't limit this collection to your professional life: feedback about your personal life can be equally powerful.

When you get mixed feedback, tease apart the positive and negative aspects. Doing so will create mental space for you to focus exclusively on the positive feedback for a concentrated period of time and to use it to build an understanding of what you should keep doing. For example, professors who receive course evaluations from hundreds of students could form a peer-coaching partnership with a trusted colleague. You would each be responsible for pulling out the positive comments from your respective course evaluations and placing them into your Kudos file.

Once you have a stash of positive feedback, set a time in your calendar to review and revisit it regularly, giving yourself the opportunity to look at it with fresh eyes. Ask yourself: What patterns or themes can I identify? What opportunities can I find to express more of my best self? What more can I learn about these strengths, and who might provide that perspective? While some people may prefer to do this on their own, it's also great to partner with a trusted friend or coach. For example, the professors in the story above could make twice-yearly early dates with a trusted colleague to share positive feedback stories and help each other interpret them and think creatively about how to incorporate what they learn into their courses.

Ask Questions

Don't just accept positive feedback; inquire into it so that you can better understand exactly how you made an impact. The key is doing this in a way that doesn't seem egotistical, allowing others to see that you are not only receptive to but grateful for their feedback.

For example, follow up on praise. We often brush off compliments, because we aren't comfortable receiving them. But they are actually an opportunity for learning—though only if they are specific and storied. Try to unpack generic labels and vague comments; seek to understand what worked well for you and for others in specific situations. Say: "Thank you for noticing X; your feedback made my day! Could you tell me what about my actions seemed to have a specific impact on you? I am trying to figure out what my strengths are so I can continue to make a positive impact at work."

During formal performance evaluations, ask for one detailed example of the strengths your manager identified. Ask too if there are any other opportunities they know of where those strengths could be used. For example, after getting feedback that "team meetings seem to go better when you are there," one professional we know asked her boss if there were other meetings where her calm presence and facilitation skills could be used to improve group conversations. Her boss realized that she could be useful at an upcoming customer forum, and a new outlet to display her strengths was born.

Research shows that managers avoid giving specific, actionable praise, so it may be up to you to make the first move in asking about the things that are going well in your job, and then probing deeply enough to get a concrete answer. For example, in a one-on-one meeting with your manager, say: "I am trying to learn more about how I contribute at work, so that I can continue to build upon and leverage these contributions. As my manager, you are likely to have the best perspective on when, where and how I make a difference in this organization. Could you give me a specific example of a time when you think I was at my best and added value to your team?"

Consider setting up a meeting with a mentor or coach to discuss only your strengths and how you can develop and leverage them for greater impact. Set up a separate discussion to talk about your developmental opportunities in your areas of weakness. Because bad feedback has a stronger hold over us than good, it is nearly impossible for you to focus on both strengths and weaknesses in the same meeting. If you provide feedback to others, consider using this practice to help your employees grow and thrive.

Study Your Successes

Conduct after-action reviews of your own work to set benchmarks and identify best practices for future work. Use the example of sports teams: review the "tape" to identify what went well, and to develop future "plays" based on what you find.

If you receive positive feedback in person, take some time after leaving that interaction to write reflectively about the experience, creating a short narrative about what you did and the impact it had. Journaling is a powerful practice, and can help you see ways in which you can bring out your best self. For example, an intellectual property director we know took up journaling to try to boost his personal and professional development. Reflecting on his entries allowed him to notice that he was best able to manage his demanding clients when he had an informal dinner with them the night before where he often got some hints about the client's interests and concerns. This client preview boosted his confidence and put him at ease and allowed him to be fully present in the more formal meetings. Once he understood this, he began holding these informal dinners more regularly—allowing his best self to come forward more consistently. This resulted in stronger relationships with clients, and ultimately a promotion.

Also take time to reflect on your strengths more generally. For example, how can your strengths complement your weaknesses? And consider the shadow side of your strengths: how can your weaknesses overpower or lead you to misapply your strengths, and how can you avoid this occurrence?

Once you make a practice of analyzing your best self by noticing positive feedback, asking questions, and studying your successes, you will develop a more holistic and cohesive understanding of the contents of your best self and the contextual factors that allow you to bring this best self into your work. The next steps help prepare you to bring this best self to life in two ways: practicing and paying it forward.

Practice Enacting Your Best Self

In particularly toxic environments, it can be hard to get any affirmation at all. Finding ways to enact your best self in these contexts can be personally empowering, especially during low points in your workweek, work year, or career. Here are some options:

Bring aspects of your best self from another domain into the workplace. Find some outlet or channel where you receive affirmation for your valued contributions. This may require you to think more broadly about your best self, going beyond the walls of your immediate work environment, and then bring what you have learned from being a valued contributor elsewhere back into your work. For example, if you are part of a religious community, alumni club, or community organization, or an organizer of neighborhood potlucks, mine these different roles for positive feedback about your strengths and contributions and import them into your work role. For example, if your family describes you as a joyful tinkerer, fixer of all broken tools and technology, consider how you might bring that to work. One of our clients received best-self feedback about organizing several large-scale events that brought different members of the community together; this helped her to see how she might use this same approach to bring together her professional stakeholders in leading a major internal change initiative.

Create space in your job for your best self to show up. If you can, craft your job so that at least one aspect of your role brings out your best self. If your job is truly difficult, find even a narrow set of tasks in which you can draw on your best self to offset the less gratifying aspects while you consider the long-term viability of your tenure. We often feel most valuable at work when we can see the impact we have on others. Therefore, finding roles and outlets that allow you to give to others at work or in your professional community is likely to be an important way to create space for your best self to show up.

When you receive negative feedback, try considering it alongside of the positive feedback stories you have in your file. Reminding yourself of how you create value will reduce your defensiveness and provide you with the self-confidence and agency you need to carefully consider opportunities to use that negative feedback for growth. Identify the aspects of your best self that will help you rise to the challenge of incorporating the wisdom within negative feedback, and discern how to progress without losing your sense of self.

Pay It Forward

The best way to remember to focus on your best self is to intentionally share rich feedback with others about theirs. This practice can invoke a norm of reciprocity, whereby this form of feedback exchange becomes customary. At the close of a project, for example, share an observation of how each member of your team made a really meaningful contribution to the team. Closing festivities are a natural place to share best-self feedback, but you can also share your thoughts through written emails or letters, or one-on-one, if your time and schedule allow.

Dale Carnegie and John Maxwell likened the process of developing people to mining for gold: you must move tons of dirt in the process, but you go in looking for the gold, not the dirt. Similarly, people who recognize and affirm others' contributions can bring out the best in themselves and others more consistently. Remember, becoming your best self and bringing out the best in others is a life-long journey. With courage, curiosity and commitment, you can use best-self development to positively transform yourself, your relationships, and your organizations.

In what way is this Takeaway "Becoming Your Best" linked to BG?

Krishna has to motivate Himself and by doing so he explains to Arjuna that He is the maifestation of the Best in every form and walk of life. This is explained in detail in the Chapter-10 of BG.

CHAPTER FIVE

Be Enlightened

"According to Vedanta, there are only two symptoms of enlightenment, just two indications that a transformation is taking place within you toward a higher consciousness. The first symptom is that you stop worrying. Things don't bother you anymore. You become light-hearted and full of joy. The second symptom is that you encounter more and more meaningful coincidences in your life, more and more synchronicities. And this accelerates to the point where you actually experience the miraculous. (quoted by Carol Lynn Pearson in Consider the Butterfly)"

— Deepak Chopra, Synchrodestiny: Harnessing the Infinite Power of Coincidence to Create Miracles

In this chapter, I will be sumarizing the earlier Takeaways described in previous chapters with reference to quotes from BG.

Here are 7 insightful verses that talk about self-realization and enlightenment.

"One who is steady, who neither gets elated in happiness nor gets depressed when faced with sadness; who is free from attachments, fear, and anger, is truly the enlightened one." (chapter 2, text 56)

The verse above speaks of a conscious person reaching this

state of stillness where he/she is not excessively swayed by external stimuli. It speaks of a state where one remains balanced and grounded at all times and perceives all events/happenings in life with the same balanced state of mind. A deeply unconscious mind is fully controlled by the external stimuli. For example, if such a mind senses anger (or any such emotion) – it immediately reacts. It has no capacity to pause, think, and respond.

A conscious mind, on the other hand, is able to anchor itself to the inner stillness and remain steady without wavering to external inputs. Thoughts and corresponding emotions (like fear, anger, joy etc.) no longer control the mind as they used to. As we grow in consciousness and as our realizations start to deepen, we start having glimpses of this still nature within us. Like what occurs during a deep meditative session when our entire being becomes still.

"*Perform your duty and abandon all attachment to success or failure. Such evenness of mind is called yoga.*" (chapter 2, text 48)

Have you ever been engrossed in an activity so deeply that you became oblivious to the outcome? This is the state of yoga as described by the above verse. If you are overly focused on the outcome, the quality of your work will suffer.

For example, if a writer is overly worried about how his/her book will be received, his writing will suffer. However, if he is completely devoted to his writing, irrespective of if or not the book becomes a success, he would have created something that he is truly proud of. Plus, his creation expands his knowledge laying the ground for future creative endeavors. Edison failed more than a thousand times in his invention of the light bulb. When he was asked about these failures, he answered, "I didn't fail 1,000 times.

The light bulb was an invention with 1,000 steps". Edison knew that his failures were as equally important as his successes and that his failures lead him toward success.

"For him who has conquered the mind, the mind is the best of friends; but for one who has failed to do so, his very mind will be the greatest enemy." (chapter 6, Text 6)

The mind is an extremely powerful tool. But if we do not learn to take control of this tool, it will start to control us. This is because the mind is simply a computing machine. Its output is conditioned by the past inputs. To be a slave to a machine that works based on past inputs is certainly not prudent. If we are not careful, it's easy to get caught in the avalanche of thoughts generated by the mind every single second and that can be quite draining and counterproductive. It's no wonder people resort to all sorts of methods to escape their minds, like drink alcohol and do drugs which can wreak havoc on their health.

So how does one conquer the mind? How does one gain control over it? The most powerful way to gain mastery over your mind is to develop self-awareness. And one of the best ways to develop self-awareness is through the practice of 'meditation', which is what the next verse is about.

"The working senses are superior to dull matter; mind is higher than the senses; intelligence is still higher than the mind; and he [the soul] is even higher than the intelligence." (chapter 3, text 42)

As sentient beings, we are superior to lifeless matter. We have a powerful mind that is able to interpret and make sense of all the sensory inputs it receives and hence our mind is superior to our senses. But even beyond the intelligence of the mind is another intelligence. This intelligence lies on a deeper level – on a cellular or atomic level. This is the intelligence that works in the background keeping our bodies and the entire universe functioning. And even beyond this intelligence is the supreme intelligence of the soul or the life energy/consciousness that resides in every one of us. This is our true nature.

"Just as a lamp in a windless place does not waver, so the disciplined mind of a yogi remains steady in meditation on the self." (chapter 6, text 19)

There are various verses in the Gita that point us towards the power of meditation. Meditation has been proposed as a method that can be used to control and discipline the mind. It has also been proposed as the path to attain self-realization. When we start to meditate, we become aware of our mind and the thoughts it generates. We become aware of our ego construct and self-beliefs accumulated over our lifetime. And this realization helps us think beyond our mind and understand our true nature which is pure consciousness.

"Whatever right or wrong action a man performs by body, mind or speech is caused by five factors which are – place of action, the performer, the senses, the endeavor and ultimately the supersoul. Therefore one who thinks of himself as the only doer, is not seeing things as they are." (chapter 18, text – 14, 15, 16)

Our ego makes us take pride in what we create, and even though there is nothing wrong with that, we must not forget that there is a superior intelligence operating in all of us and our creativity comes forth through this intelligence. When we think of our creations and achievements in this manner, we become free from our egotistic minds and get in touch with our higher nature. Many great creators have expressed that when they create, they are often in a meditative state.

The famous mathematician Ramanujan who used to dish out extremely complicated equations in a matter of seconds used to say that when he was writing these equations, ideas came into him from a supreme being and that he got into a divine state. This is happening to each one of us. The only thing is we do not acknowledge it very often.

"*That knowledge by which one undivided spiritual nature is seen in all existences, undivided in the divided, is knowledge in the mode of goodness.*" (chapter 18, text 20)

This verse from the Gita directs us towards the realization of that one life energy that connects us all. On a physical level, our mind perceives separate bodies and personalities. But as we become more and more conscious, we get past the physical and see the bond that connects each one of us together. This understanding can help us break free from the narrow visions of our mind.

9 798886 062366

Printed by Libri Plureos GmbH in Hamburg,
Germany